Your Book:
The Ultimate
Business Card

First Printing 2014

Printed in the United States of America

ISBN: 978-1500600839

Other Books by the Author

7 Steps Every First Time Franchise Buyer Should Follow

Register This Book to Get Free Updates and Free Videos

To get updates to this book, access to new videos that will show you how to implement the strategies in this book, and to reach me personally, visit:

- www.UltimateBusinessCardGuide.com or
- text UBC to 58885 or
- text your name and email to (858) 683-8820

Your Book:
The Ultimate
Business Card

How to Increase Your
Visibility, Authority, and
Profits by Publishing Your
Book in Less Than 90 Days

Mark C. Leonard

Table of Contents

About the Author

Mark Leonard has a wide variety of business experience. He put himself through Davidson College in North Carolina by starting and running a landscape business. After obtaining his MBA from the Darden School at the University of Virginia, he moved out West, where he has lived ever since. He first lived in South Lake Tahoe, where he invested in real estate, and started a real estate videotaping company. That got wiped out in the early '80s as interest rates spiked to 18%, so he moved to the San Francisco Bay Area. There he landed a job at ROLM Corporation, holding positions in corporate finance, project management, and sales. He then held senior positions in a number of software companies involved in the chip design market, followed by a stint as a retained recruiter in the professional services arena. Following that, he and his wife invested in Subway™ franchises, building a new store in San Francisco's Financial District, and buying two existing stores. He sold those stores after five years and wrote a book about that experience, revealing information that is typically very difficult to obtain.

When not serving clients and studying the rapidly evolving technologies that comprise the online experience, Mark and his wife lovingly take care of their rescued greyhounds, share home cooked meals with most ingredients from their garden or the local farmers markets, and they also spend time on the water as members of the Corinthian Yacht Club, where Mark was Commodore in 2013.

Mark is now focused on helping small businesses increase their visibility and authority throughout the world by using the latest technologies.

Mark can be reached at (858) 683-8820, or by filling out the form at www.UltimateBusinessCardGuide.com.

Introduction

If you are an expert in your field, and you want more visibility and more high-value clients, then this book is for you. I will show you how to author and publish your unique message in the form of a book quickly and easily. Not only that, the book will be offered by one of the biggest brands in the world: Amazon®! If you are an expert who works with clients who spend a lot of money with you, think about the value you could bring to your market if you were able, within the next 3 months, to hand your highest value prospects your book that effectively delivers the message you would like to communicate. Could you secure more speaking engagements in front of targeted groups? Could you close more prospects? Could you increase your bottom line?

Publishing your own book can be an important component of your overall marketing effort, and can certainly complement your other efforts. It's not meant to replace your online and face-to-face networking, or the effective advertising you may be doing, but it can certainly help those efforts. And by having a book that communicates your message, it can help smooth out your business flow by providing a constant stream of qualified prospects. It can also help shorten your time to deal closure, and provide you with prospects who are more knowledgeable and therefore easier to work with.

Getting your book written and published isn't particularly technically challenging these days, but it does require single-minded focus and a methodology. If you do want to publish your own book, this book will help you choose whether to do it all yourself, or whether you would benefit from having others help you.

This book isn't necessarily intended for fiction or non-fiction authors who want to make a living from selling their books. The basics contained in the book are all applicable in that case, but making money from writing books will require other skills that aren't contained in this book.

That's why the book is titled "Your Book: Your Ultimate Business Card": its purpose is to help you get known, and get your message out to a wider circle of prospects. If you are ready to publish your own book, read on!

1 | Why Publish a Book?

Your Ultimate Business Card

As a professional who has deep expertise in your area and who is seeking new clients, you have a big challenge. Take a moment to put yourself in the shoes of your best prospects. Although you have the right amount of experience and expertise to provide the products and/or services your prospects need, they don't know that yet. You also know they have many choices where they can find out about the product or service you provide: personal friends, researching the internet, scanning social media, consulting with trusted advisors, and seeing advertising.

How are YOU going to stand out?

You have a lot of ways to get your message out and reach your ideal prospects.

- You have a business card: so do all your competitors.

- You have a good website: so do all your competitors.

- You do some advertising: most of your competitors do too.

- You participate in networking groups: so do most of your competitors.

- You have your profile up on LinkedIn®: so do your competitors.

- You participate in industry conventions and workshops: so do your competitors.

What if you were an author and handed or sent your prospect your book? The book is authoritative, well-written, interesting to read, and most of all, provides your prospect with relevant, useful, actionable information. How many of your competitors have **that** in their arsenal? Not many.

No question about it: being the author of your own book gives you competitive differentiation.

Being a published author gives you **instant credibility**. Everybody knows it's not easy to organize your knowledge into a readable book, and the fact that you have prioritized your effort to write a book instantly differentiates you from most, if not all, of your competitors.

It provides visible, physical proof that you can take on a complex project and get it finished. Not everyone can do that.

Having your own well-written book establishes **trust that you are an authority in your field**. Think about it: the root of authority is "author".

Having your own book also enables you to **strengthen your branding**. As a successful professional, you have a unique set of skills and knowledge that has enabled your success in the marketplace. You have established your brand. Articulating that knowledge in a book reinforces that brand, and can help you propel your business to the next level.

Plus, being an author is going to be **cool to talk about at cocktail parties**. Who knows, you could end up with new prospects, or other connections. It could change your life!

The bottom line is authoring a book has a high likelihood of enabling you to **make more money**, and **enjoy more success**, however you define that. That is why publishing your own book is your Ultimate Business Card.

Generate New Business

Authoring your own book is very likely to help you generate new business. How you use your book in your overall marketing effort is limited only by your creativity, but here are a couple of ideas that should get you started. Chapter 5 gives more specifics, but here are some general ideas.

First, when you get your book published, it's a great time to **reach out to your past clients**, and let them know you've written a book, and offer to send it to them, ideally for free. You'll also want to encourage them to write a review of the book online if they are so inclined.

You'll also want to encourage them to share the book with others who may also want your services, and you can even offer to send them additional books at no cost. Sending these books may **remind your past clients that they should consider hiring you again**. For example, if you are an estate attorney who drafted an estate plan for a client several years ago, receiving the book may remind them that it's time to update their estate plan because things have changed.

The other benefit this approach has is that it will **stimulate word-of-mouth advertising**, which is generally regarded as the gold standard for advertising effectiveness.

Another way that a book can generate new business is to encourage readers who like your content to join your community. You should make it clear throughout your book how to reach you, and have more interaction with you.

One of the other ways that your book can generate new business is the **"lumpy mail"** technique. In today's environment of so much communication occurring online, sending a "lumpy package" to a prospect with a personal inscription may very well earn you additional clients. Again, how many of your competitors do this?

Another way your book can help you generate new business is to **shorten the sales cycle**. If your book clearly explains your differentiating factors, and educates your prospective clients about how they can apply your knowledge to benefit themselves, they will likely be easier to close after they have gone through your book, and will also be easier to work with after you have earned their business.

More Speaking, Writing, and Consulting

Once you have your book published, now is the time to leverage the book to obtain more opportunities to speak to groups interested in your subject, and to get invitations to write in other publications, both online and offline. Those speaking and writing occasions will then lead to the possibility of additional consulting and sales opportunities.

Do you participate actively in a professional or networking group? If so, once you have your book available, start calling the people responsible for booking speakers at the conferences they organize, and let them know about your book, and your availability as a speaker. Then, at the events where you are speaking, you can either sell your books, or give them away in return for getting names and email addresses of the recipients.

You'll also want to use your book to open doors to other publications. Many content publishers, whether local newspaper, regional or national magazine, or popular bloggers are all looking for original content. Announcing that you have written a book that may be of interest to their readers will often result in an invitation to write for their publication.

All of these speaking and writing opportunities are likely to lead to new consulting gigs, or sales of your products.

The other way to use your new book as leverage is to repurpose the content. If the content is originally written for the book, you can record and post videos online, break the subjects down to write articles, blog posts, newsletter content, to add pages to your website, and more.

Share Your Passion

Another purpose in publishing your book may simply be to share your passion for your subject. Since you are a subject matter expert, it's likely that you have developed know-how or insights that very few others on the planet know about or can duplicate.

Sharing your skills will help others achieve results that they otherwise might not be able to duplicate, and in this way, you can make the world a better place.

In addition, teaching others about your field of knowledge opens the door to having you increase your own knowledge level and expertise as you begin to network with other experts in your field. Putting out a book that gives value enables you create a community of like-minded people who can help each other.

One of the great joys of being a self-published author is that there is a very supportive community of other authors who really enjoy sharing their trials and successes, and encouraging others.

Make a Little Money

This section is deliberately last. The primary purpose of this book is to encourage professionals or experts with specialized knowledge how to get their first books published quickly, and to use their books to improve their professional results.

As such, this book isn't written so much for the person who wants to write books as a source of passive income. This is certainly a possibility, and with the rapid deployment of self-publishing technologies, more people than ever have cracked the code on writing for a living. But this isn't easy, and demands a whole new set of skills for which there are many books and courses. However, it is likely that if your subject area has broad regional, national or global appeal, by getting your book out there, and following much of the advice in this book, you may be able to generate a little bit of extra income from sales of the book.

To get updates to this book, access to new videos that will show you how to implement the strategies in this book, and to reach me personally, visit:

- *www.UltimateBusinessCardGuide.com or*
- *text UBC to 58885 or*
- *text your name and email to (858) 683-8820*

2 | Why Self-Publish?

Easy

Well, yes and no. The fact is that it's not too difficult for an average person who is reasonably computer literate to get a book self-published. The hardest part is the writing: getting the book organized, thinking through the message that you want to create, getting the content into the written word, and then editing and proofreading the copy.

And while getting the content created is probably the most time-consuming part, there are still a lot of other intricate details to get right in order to produce a book that you will be proud to have your name on. Chapter 4 discusses these in detail, but if you are going to do these steps yourself, count on spending 20-40 hours at a minimum (not including writing, editing, and proofreading your content) for learning how to get the layout just right for both your hard copy book and your eBook, converting your content to the right file type for uploading, designing a pleasing front and back cover, deciding on pricing, setting up your accounts and entering all your information, writing and entering all the meta information you will need to provide, which I cover in more detail in Chapter 4, and then proofing the final copy.

If you are publishing your book as your Ultimate Business Card, that simplifies the process. You will do just fine to create a high quality paperback book using Amazon's CreateSpace®, and then convert the book to Kindle® format for your ebook publishing. Yes, there are many other options out there for you, including Lulu™, Xlibris™, Blurb™, and many more in the print-on-demand sector, and for eBooks, you have your choice of Apple®, Google®, Sony eReader®, Barnes and Noble Nook® and Smashwords® formats, and others, but you probably don't need to worry about skipping these if your main purpose is to create your Ultimate Business Card.

Of course, the easiest way to get all this done is to delegate any or all of the work to a self-publishing assistance service. This will certainly cost more than doing it yourself, but it will be faster, and certainly require much less effort on your part. Plus, frankly, others who specialize in these tasks will probably be able to produce more professional results. There are a virtually unlimited range of options out there, including services provided by Amazon, and costs can range from several hundred dollars to well into five figures, depending on who you select and what services you want.

What is surprising to many prospective authors is how many books are ghost written, and this is a real possibility for you, especially if you don't have the desire, time, or skills to write a complete book. I discuss this option more thoroughly in Chapter 4.

Fast Time to Market

One of the reasons that self-publishing is becoming so popular is that it completely bypasses the agony of the traditional publishing marketplace, and enables an author to get their book out within weeks, instead of years. This is especially important if your primary purpose in publishing is to create your Ultimate Business Card.

The promise of this book is that you can have your book in your hands within four to twelve weeks from the time you commit to the project, even if you haven't yet written a single word.

Inexpensive

The initial cost of creating an Ultimate Business Card book from scratch can range from less than $50 if you do all of the work yourself, up to $3,000-$15,000 or more for "done-for-you" publishing services. Once your book is written, getting a standard 6" x 9" formatted paperback book that is roughly 12,000-20,000 words is going to cost a little over $3.00 each plus shipping, delivered to your door in the continental US, in quantities as small as one book.

You Retain All Rights

Because you are self-publishing, and either doing or paying for all the services (writing, print-on-demand, etc.), you retain full rights to all your content. In the old-school world of traditional publishing, a previously unpublished writer typically gives up the copyright for five to seven years, and gets a 5-8% royalty.

Control

Because you are publishing yourself, all of the decisions regarding content, layout, titling, cover design, pricing, distribution, and marketing are in your hands. You can do all this yourself, or subcontract out the parts that you want professional help with. Even if you do contract out for some services, the final decisions and product is still yours.

Mutual Support

It's pretty well known that the world of very popular traditionally published authors is cutthroat. Gore Vidal famously said "Whenever a friend succeeds, a little something in me dies."

That is definitely not the case with the self-published author community. There are many online and local groups that encourage each other and provide mutual support.

Higher Royalties

If you are "lucky" enough to get picked up by a traditional publisher, you will likely get 5-8% royalties on any sales made (if any). When you self-publish, you can set your own pricing and determine your own royalty level. The way CreateSpace calculates royalties is that they take the per-page cost of the book plus $0.85 off the top (for books greater than 110 pages), plus deduct 40% of the selling price, and the author gets whatever is left.

Example: Let's say you have written a 184 page book, printed black & white, and you priced it at $9.99.

$9.99 – Sales Price

-4.00 – 40% distribution fee (US)

-0.85 – Fixed Fee

-2.20 – Per page cost

$2.94 – Royalty to Author (29%)

And of course you can buy as many books as you want for yourself at about $3 each.

For eBooks distributed through Kindle, you can choose to receive a 35% or 70% royalty, depending on other choices you make. If, on the above book, you set the Kindle price to $7.99, and you choose the 70% option, you would receive $5.60 for each sale.

To get updates to this book, access to new videos that will show you how to implement the strategies in this book, and to reach me personally, visit:

- *www.UltimateBusinessCardGuide.com or*
- *text UBC to 58885 or*
- *text your name and email to (858) 683-8820*

3 | Challenges to Self-Publishing

While the actual process of self-publishing is not too technically difficult, there are nevertheless a lot of challenges.

Writing

Journalist Gene Fowler said: "Writing is easy: All you do is sit staring at a blank sheet of paper until drops of blood form on your forehead." In that sense, and for most people, writing ain't easy!

On the other hand, there are now so many ways to write that it CAN be easy. I discuss these options thoroughly in Chapter 4.

Intimidating

There is no doubt that writing AND publishing a book is a significant project, with many different tasks to complete in order to produce the finished product. The author has to decide on the audience, the message, the voice used in writing the book, how to organize the content, write the content, edit the content, decide on book formats, choose a title, design a cover, proofread the final version, set up accounts with print-on-demand and/or ebook publishers, get it published, then start marketing the book. For many would-be authors, especially busy professionals, this is an intimidating process.

Self-Confidence

If you don't define yourself primarily as an author, the thought of writing a book can certainly evoke fear and a lack of confidence. Exposing your thoughts and ideas, not to mention your writing skills, in a publically available format causes most people, and even some published authors, a lot of angst. And if an author lacks confidence, the project is either going to take a very long time to complete, or never get done.

Editing

Once the structure is organized, and the bulk of the writing is complete, there is still a great deal of work to be done. Even if you don't have aspirations that the book will be read by millions of people, it is still important that the writing appear professional. That requires editing, often by an outside professional, and there are several levels to editing, which I discuss in detail in Chapter 4. I call the first part "Chainsaw Editing", but it's known in publishing circles as developmental editing, which is making sure that the high level messaging is clear, and the book is structured to support the message. The next level of editing, called copy editing, then checks for proper usage of the language, including grammar and spelling errors. Production editing formats the content for the medium, i.e., ebook, paperback, or hardback. Finally, the book needs to be proofread carefully in each medium before finally being published.

Making It Interesting

No matter how dry or technical the subject matter is, the writing needs to be engaging to the reader, especially if the primary purpose of the book is to market or explain the products or services provided by the author. Making writing interesting is always a challenge, even for experienced authors.

Professional Appearance

Unfortunately, many self-published books reveal themselves to be amateur productions when there are many misspellings, formatting inconsistencies, too many fonts, odd page numbers on the left pages, and other signals that the work of the book hasn't been carefully reviewed. This can damage the credibility of the author, even if the content of the book is otherwise excellent.

Cover Design

The phrase "You can't judge a book by its cover" may be true, but if a book has a poor cover, even potentially interested readers will avoid reading the book. Many books which have moved up the charts in Amazon started out underperforming until the cover got redesigned in a way that connected with readers. Designing a good cover truly is an art, and almost always needs to be done by a graphics professional.

Formatting

The completed manuscript is only the beginning of the publishing process. The self-publishing author then needs to decide on the trim size, which is publishing language for page size, of the hard copy books, and format the book appropriately. The book needs to be reformatted as an ebook acceptable to ebook publishers, such as Amazon's Kindle, Barnes and Noble's Nook, Sony's eReader, and so on. The front pages need to be created and numbered appropriately, the correct font type and size need to be selected, and the Table of Contents needs to be properly created.

Again, these are tasks that aren't necessarily too technically difficult, but are tedious and require a lot of care and attention to detail.

Good Title

This task is almost as challenging and as important as designing a good cover. It needs to quickly and clearly communicate the main value of the book to the reader, and needs to be attention-getting and interesting without forcing the reader to think too hard about what the contents of the book contain. Coming up with a good title is almost always challenging.

Creating Metadata

In the self-publishing world, there are a number of tasks other than writing pure content that need to be completed as part of the publishing process. These include a book description that will be displayed online where the book is offered for sale, as well as an "About the Author" paragraph. Other metadata include selecting the BISAC (Book Industry Standards and Communications) category, and listing the keywords or categories that would enable people searching for the book to find the work.

Marketing

It should be clear from the beginning of the writing process how the book will be marketed once it is published. Even if the main purpose of the book is to act as your Ultimate Business Card, you should develop a written plan for how the book will be used to fulfill that purpose. This plan can be simple, but the act of creating the plan may stimulate ideas about how the book can be used. For example, you might want to announce the publication in your LinkedIn profile and on Facebook® and Twitter®, you might want to create videos to distribute on YouTube® and Google+, you might want to issue a press-release or two, you might want to send copies of the book to conference organizers where you would like to speak, you might send copies to your existing clients, add some content about the book on your website, etc. And of course, send the book to prospective clients. Thinking through and creating a marketing plan is challenging, but well worth the effort.

To get updates to this book, access to new videos that will show you how to implement the strategies in this book, and to reach me personally, visit:

- *www.UltimateBusinessCardGuide.com or*
- *text UBC to 58885 or*
- *text your name and email to (858) 683-8820*

4 | How to Self-Publish in Less Than 90 Days

Getting a book written, edited, formatted, and published in four to twelve weeks is aggressive, but doable with enough focus and probably with the help of qualified professionals. However, the timeframe is secondary to producing a high-quality book and completing the following tasks should produce a book that will please most authors and readers.

Define Purpose and Expectations

Start with taking some time to clearly define the reason for committing to writing a book. Publishing a book is a time-consuming project, so investing time up front to get a clear picture of what you want to accomplish with the book is extremely important.

Answering the following questions will help with getting the purpose and expectations defined.

- **Who is the audience for the book?** Is it your prospective client who doesn't yet know who you are? Is it your referral network that you want to help educate about the range of your services? It might be very useful to even invent one or two "avatars" at this point. An avatar is an imaginary creation that has the characteristics of your target audience. Be specific: provide a name, age, gender, description, and profile. For example, if you are selling real estate, your avatar might be Linda, who works in mid-level management in the local school district, and who is a 43-year-old single mom with a twelve-year-old daughter and ten-year-old son. As you write content, pretend to have a conversation with Linda about your subject matter. This will make it a lot easier for you to create that content. You don't need to restrict yourself to a single avatar: there could be a couple, but not too many, or the message will start to get garbled.

- **What are the primary challenges that your prospective reader has that you can help solve?** There is a phenomenon known to people with deep expertise called "the curse of knowledge." What this means is that the expert tends to forget the mindset of their prospective clients who have little knowledge of the subject area. Spend some time thinking about and writing down the primary problem that you solve using your expertise. What are your prospects, or avatars, struggling with when you talk with them?

- **What are the immediate benefits that you think you can get by publishing the book?** This may be the most important consideration of all. If the projected benefits are relatively minor, it may not be worth the time or money to work on writing and publishing a book. On the other hand, if the benefits are significant, that could provide the extra motivation needed to take the project to completion. Some of the benefits of becoming a published author were highlighted in Chapter 1, and include:

    - Instant credibility, leading to more sales

    - Badge of authority, leading to appearances on speaking and writing circuits

    - Educating prospective clients, leading to shorter sales cycles and better service after the sale

    - Competitive differentiation, where you are the only professional in your immediate marketplace who is an author

An expectation that might **not** be particularly useful is the hope of making a lot of money by selling books online. Even with the explosion in the selling of eBooks, and the ease of publishing books from print-on-demand providers, relatively few authors make a lot of money from their writing, especially with just one book. However, it is relatively easy to get your book on Amazon, and you may get some sales that help offset some of the costs of creating the book.

Create Marketing Plan

If your book is well-targeted, and has answers for challenges faced by your readers, having a written marketing plan will accelerate the results you get when the book is published. Here are some suggestions to get started on a marketing plan:

- **Online Videos.** Create a series of short (two to seven minutes each) videos about your content, then post these to your YouTube channel, and embed them on your website blog.

- **Press Release.** Send out a press-release announcing the book. Using a service like PRWeb® or PRNewswire® is helpful, but also be sure to send the release to local newspapers and trade periodicals.

- **Social Media.** Be sure to announce your book's availability on LinkedIn, and on your Facebook and Twitter accounts, and any other social media accounts you use.

- **Website.** Be sure to announce the book on your website, along with a link to the eBook or hardcopy retailer.

- **Blog Content.** Take some of the content from your book and write blog posts about it.

- **Newsletter.** If you have a newsletter, be sure to send out an announcement to everyone on your list, perhaps offering to send anyone who asks a free copy.

- **Referral Network.** Reach out to your network that you trade leads with and let them know the book is available. Send those in your network a free copy upon request.

- **Prospects.** Send a copy of your book to prospects as a "lumpy package," along with a sales letter, inviting them to engage in a conversation with you.

- **Conference Organizers.** If you want to speak at shows or conferences attended by prospective clients, make a list of these conferences, send a book to the people who organize the conferences, and let them know you are available.

- **Speaking Engagements.** Be sure to bring copies of your book to sell or give away when you get invited to speak.

- **Guest Blog.** Offer to guest post on related blogs. Reach out to other gurus in your marketplace and offer to write content on their blog.

Research

Go to Amazon and look for other books that have been written in your subject matter area. Create a spreadsheet that has the following information:

- Book Title
- Book Author
- Publication Date
- Paperback Price (if applicable)
- Paperback Pages (if applicable)
- Kindle Price (if applicable)
- Number of Reviews
- Amazon Rank

Having this information at your fingertips will help you understand what is resonating with your readers, how popular the subject is, what pricing should be, and also may give you ideas on what your title could be. Be sure to read some of the reviews, especially some of the negative reviews, to discover what is missing from other books in the field. If you can provide content that is missing in other books, you will gain more followers.

Draft Table of Contents

Now the real work begins. Getting the content into a document will be the most challenging and time consuming task. The good news is that there are many ways to get this done, both by yourself, or with the help of professionals. Your goal should be to create a manuscript with a minimum of 12,000 words. 18,000 to 25,000 words is an excellent length that will provide enough "heft" in a typical paperback to establish credibility, but not so lengthy that readers would be afraid of starting to examine the contents.

Writing out the Table of Contents should start with the definition of the purpose of the book that we created earlier. Here's a trick to help you generate that table of contents. Keeping in mind who your audience is, write down the top ten "Frequently Asked Questions (FAQs)" that you get. Now, write down the top ten questions that your prospects **should** be asking you (SAQs), but may not have the knowledge to articulate. You can write these down in a document editor or a spreadsheet, but I like to use mindmapping. For a free version of a mindmapping software program that I really like, go to http://xmind.net. Your FAQs and SAQs now become your chapters.

Next, for each chapter, write down two or three sentences that go a little deeper into each question or topic.

Finally, prioritize the topics, or chapters, in a way that brings a flow to the topics. Now you have a table of contents, with subtopics, that will enable you to write faster.

Choose Hardcopy and/or eBook

There are so many options for self-publishing these days, and one of the first decisions you should make as you move towards publishing your Ultimate Business Card is whether you want to publish in hardcopy, ebook, or both.

The advantage of printing a hardcopy book, which can be either hardbound or paperback, is that many people still prefer to have a physical manifestation of a book that they can hold and read. Since your primary purpose is to use your book as your Ultimate Business Card, having a hardcopy book enables you to send, sell, or give a physical item to a prospect. Hardcopy books are also more flexible to design just the way you want. I recommend that you create a hardcopy book.

Furthermore, I recommend that you make your Ultimate Business Card into a black and white paperback. They are very inexpensive and quick to produce, and it is what your readers probably expect.

There are many hardcopy printers who will print your books on demand, known as print-on-demand, or POD. Printers you may have heard of include Lightning Books®, Lulu, Blurb, and my recommendation, Amazon's CreateSpace.

CreateSpace is relatively easy to set up and publish in, they have a variety of industry standard trim sizes, they are inexpensive and fast. Finally, it's also very easy to get the book into the Amazon catalog, which still has a dominant market share, especially for non-fiction works.

And finally, to make it even easier for you, I recommend a trim size of a standard 6" x 9" form, with a glossy cover, and white paper.

The next question is whether to simultaneously publish your book in ebook format. The downside is that there is additional formatting work to make your book ready for ebook publishing. Then you need to make pricing decisions on both the hardcopy version and the electronic version. Generally, the additional effort is not too challenging, and I recommend that you give your readers a choice by also producing an ebook version.

Here again, there are a number of possibilities for publishing your ebook, including Barnes and Noble's Nook, Sony Reader, Kobu®, Apple's iBook®, and Amazon's Kindle. I recommend that you publish your eBook in Kindle format, and I'll discuss that topic further in the "Set Up Accounts" section.

Write the Content Yourself

Since you are reading this book, you probably don't have a fully written book hiding somewhere on your hard-drive. If you do, now would be the time to open it up, see how well it matches your purpose, and begin editing. The remainder of this book will help you transform your work into a fully published book.

However, if you are like most experts, you may have written articles, reports, white papers, website content or blog posts in the past that may serve as the content for some of your chapters. If you do have this content available, be sure to review it now, and keep it in mind as you begin to write the book content. You may be able to use that content directly, or with some minor editing.

If you are essentially starting from scratch, there are several ways to get the book written. If you are a capable writer, and you like the writing process, including using word processing, then here's a tip to help you get that book written:

Suggested Action: Put your writing time on your calendar as appointments with yourself.

For most writers, it is important to go into a state of intense concentration with no distractions. Turn your phone off, make sure your calendar is clear and that you have uninterrupted time. You will quickly learn how long you can write before you need to take a break, and how many hours per day and words per day you can write. Once you have that information, put enough time on your schedule to complete your book.

If you have a well-organized table of contents, you will probably find that you can write 500-1,000 words per hour, maybe faster. Therefore, a 20,000-word book would take you 20-40 hours to write. If you schedule that time, then you have some degree of confidence to set a deadline when the book is ready for editing.

But here's what is important: you should enjoy the process. If you don't, it's likely that the book won't get written, or that it will take too long, or you won't be happy with it.

Get the Content Ghost Written

If you find that you don't have the time, patience, discipline, or aptitude for writing your own book, there is another way: get someone else to write it!

There are ghost-writers all over the world, and the costs can vary from a few hundred dollars to tens of thousands of dollars, and the quality can vary just as much. There is no one way to find the ghost-writer that is best for your project. Possible sources include Odesk®, eLance®, even Fiverr®, and you can find many sources online by Googling "ghost writer". You can also post an ad on Craigslist® or at a local college or university.

There are many ways to structure your agreement with a ghost-writer. They might charge you by the word, by the project, or by the hour. They might agree to do a fair amount of research, or they might only rely on notes or recorded interviews with you. They may or may not be willing or able to help you with high level (developmental) editing or even proofreading. In any event, when you hire a ghost-writer, you retain the copyright to the words. It is important that this be in your contract with your writer.

You will find that the more organized you are, the smoother the ghost writing will go. That is why it is so important to have a well-conceived table of contents, and the bones of some content for each chapter.

In my business, I provide complete ghost-writing using a method that can usually be fun and minimize the amount of time my clients need to spend on the project. Once we have the table of contents written and agreed upon, we schedule a series of phone interviews, which we record. We go through each chapter and get you to talk about that particular topic. I then have the recordings transcribed, and the content is then ready for editing.

Of course, this is a process that you can do yourself. You could record the content onto your smartphone, or onto your computer using audio recording software (Audacity™ is a free program that I sometimes use), and then send the resulting audio file to a transcription service. Generally, you will pay about $1.00 - $2.00 per minute for the transcript.

How much time does it take the client? The average is about 8,000 words per hour, so a 16,000 word book would take about 2 hours of your time for the interviews, which can be done all at once if you have a lot of stamina, or it can be broken up into segments. In general, somewhere between a 30 and 60 minute interval seems to work for most people.

Create and Add Images

During the writing process, you may find it helpful to add illustrations, diagrams, tables, and/or photos that contribute to the clarity of the text. If so, now is the time to determine what items you want, where they will go, what you want them to show, and what captions they will have.

For drawings and illustrations, you'll want to get these professionally drawn, unless you are an accomplished graphics artist. Sketch out what you have in mind, then find an artist to create a high resolution image, generally a jpg with a minimum resolution of 300 dpi (dots per inch). Be sure that the image size fits within the page dimension that you choose. Also, you will want to keep your images in black and white, or grayscale, in order to keep your costs down.

Tables can be added easily to CreateSpace paperbacks, but again it is important to keep their dimensions inside the dimensions you have set for your book. It is trickier with Kindle, and here the easiest method is to save a table as a high-resolution image, and insert it.

Photos can be added and should be converted to grayscale if they are in color, and should be at least 300 dpi.

"Chainsaw" Editing

Once the rough text of the content is written, it's time to step back and do your high-level editing, which I like to call chainsaw editing. The purpose of chainsaw, or developmental, editing is to make sure that the book is well-organized, coherent, readable, and complete. This level of editing is most often done by a third party editor who may be able to see things and make suggestions that the author is just too close to notice. Here are some of the questions that a developmental editor will review:

- Is the book well organized? Does it have a good flow?

- Does the content consistently address the needs of the reader, as defined by the "avatar"?

- Are there topics or subjects that need to be added or expanded upon? Is the book complete?

- Are there topics that can be deleted or compressed without harming the overall goal of the book?

- Is the language clear and articulate?

- Is the use of Figures and Exhibits consistent, informative, and are they correctly identified?

- Is the tone and style consistent?

- In retrospect, does the content and organization communicate to your reader the overall message that you wanted to communicate when you wrote the table of contents?

Write Front Matter

Open any traditionally published book or any carefully self-published book, and you will find varying quantities of preliminary information, generally referred to as "front matter." Here are some items that you'll want to consider for front matter for your book, and they are listed in the usual order that they should appear in your book.

- **Reviews.** Known as "blurbs" in the publishing world, these are brief reviews by readers who have had an opportunity to read the book in advance and have written brief testimonials about the book. Sometimes these are paid, and sites like Kirkus Indie® and Foreword Clarion® will charge $300-600 for a review. While having reviews is completely optional, there is no doubt that reviews are very helpful if you intend to build an independent audience for the book outside your direct network. If you have a network of people to whom you can send copies of the book before it is published, especially leaders in your industry, and entice them to write reviews, that can be very helpful.

- **Half title.** A half title, usually at the front of the book, is a page that has only the main title of the publication. The subtitle and author's name are omitted in this page of the front matter. The half title page should be on the right side of the book.

- **Other Books by the Author.** If you have written other books, a list of those books is useful information to the reader, and certainly adds to your credibility.

- **Title page.** A title page has, at a minimum, the full title of the work, including the subtitle (if any), and the name of the author(s), contributors (if applicable), illustrators (if applicable), and, optionally, the publisher's name and website address.

- **Copyright information.** This has the copyright notice, the date the book was written, and usually a sentence or two establishing the copyright terms.

- **Date of publication.** This is usually associated with the copyright information.

- **Edition notice.** You might want to state that this is your first edition, or, if it is a subsequent edition, you might want to indicate the significant changes you made in subsequent editions.

- **ISBN.** This acronym stands for International Standards Book Number, and is a unique 13-digit number that identifies your book. In the United States, the company authorized to issue ISBNs is RR Bowker®. Numbers can be obtained for $125 each, or $250 for a block of 10. While it isn't imperative to have an ISBN, it's a good idea. For your Ultimate Business Card book, where I use Amazon's CreateSpace as my Print on Demand provider, they provide ISBNs for free. The only downside to this is that CreateSpace is listed as the publisher. Most readers couldn't care less, so I recommend going this route, but if you want to establish your own publishing brand, you should buy ISBNs from RR Bowker. Also, the ISBN is almost always created in barcode format and placed on the back cover in the lower right.

Each new version of your book requires its own ISBN, so the ISBN for a paperback, a hardcover copy, and an eBook (if you choose one) would all be different ISBNs. Amazon's Kindle publishing division, Kindle Direct Publishing®, does not offer ISBNs for its Kindle books, but does mandate that the author NOT use the ISBN from any hardcopy books. Bowker, of course, argues that having an ISBN on all books is important, but many authorities in the self-publishing world do not think it is important.

- **LCCN.** LCCN, which stands for Library of Congress Catalog Number, is a numerical cataloging system for the US Library of Congress. If you plan to sell your book to libraries you'll want an LCCN. The good news is that applying for an LCCN is free. First, you need to set up an account through the website of the Cataloging in Publication Division of the Library of Congress (http://www.loc.gov/publish/cip) by giving them an ISBN that you own, which establishes you as a publisher. After the account is approved, you request the LCCN which will record the information for your book. When the book is published you will be required to send two copies of the book to the Library of Congress to be filed with the number.

- **About the Author.** This is a bio that establishes why the reader will want to read your book, and more importantly, provides an opportunity to direct the reader to your website, Facebook page, LinkedIn profile, or other ways to get in touch with you, such as your phone number or email address. This should include a grayscale photo.

- **Dedication.** A dedication is a part of the front matter that is written by the author and includes the names of the person/persons the author wishes to honor. This is very common in works of fiction, but completely optional for non-fiction books.

- **Table of Contents.** A table of contents (ToC) is typically in the middle of the front matter. It may be a very short and simple listing of the chapters of the book, or it may be very detailed, including subchapters. It is generally created automatically in your word processing program by setting up chapter titles and subtitles as "styles", and then you can specify how many levels you want to display in the ToC. In your hardcopy version, you'll want to reference the page numbers, but in the eBook version, you'll want it to only link to the chapters, so you'll want to suppress page numbers.

- **Acknowledgements.** Another part of front matter is an acknowledgement, which is written by the author and acknowledges those who have helped him/her in the writing of the publication. This section can also go at the end of the book in the "back matter." In a Kindle eBook, you'll want to include this at the back because Amazon provides a "Look Inside" peek at about the first 10% of the book, and you'd rather have your potential readers read real content.

- **Foreword.** A foreword is an essay, or short piece of writing, written by someone other than the author, and ideally a well-known authority in your field. It often explains the relationship between the writer of the foreword and either the author or the story being told. If you can get a leader in your field to write your foreword, that helps establish your credibility.

- **Preface/Introduction.** A preface is an introduction to the book that is written by the author. It usually covers how and why the publication came into being, where the idea for the book came from, and what the purpose and goals are in writing the book.

Write Back Matter

The "back matter" refers to information contained after the main content is finished. Much of this optional, but if done thoughtfully, can increase the value of the book for the reader. Here are the main sections.

- **Conclusion**. Sometimes it is helpful to wrap up the book with a conclusion that helps the reader summarize the benefits that the book provides.

- **Index**. Although this is optional, many non-fiction works, especially those that deal with somewhat technical topics, benefit from having a well-written index. This can be very tedious work, but fortunately there are many contractors who are willing to take on this task relatively inexpensively. This is more helpful in printed books, as the Find function in eBooks can help the reader find any content they want.

- **Resources**. Throughout your book, you may very well reference outside companies, organizations, websites, and people. Having a listing in the back of the book adds nice value for the reader. Again, it's not as necessary in eBooks because links to the listed resources can be embedded in the eBook itself.

- **Glossary**. A glossary is especially helpful if the subject is reasonably technical and/or contains a lot of acronyms. The glossary is usually created manually, as most commonly used word processing programs don't have a clean simple way of creating a glossary automatically.

- **Bibliography**. A bibliography is more likely to be used in a heavily researched book, and therefore may not be needed in an Ultimate Business Card book.

- **Disclaimers/Warranties.** If you have written a book that contains financial, medical, or business advice you might want to have a paragraph or two that establishes that you aren't responsible for any results the reader achieves after reading your book. Consult with a qualified attorney to get this language. While this section is often found in the Front Matter, I recommend that it be in back because Amazon's "Look Inside" feature displays the first 10% and you want to make it juicy content, not the legal warnings.

- **Appendices**. These can consolidate useful information in a format that the reader can readily access. The Resources section might be in an appendix, as could be a list of objects that you have in the book. For example, in my book "7 Steps Every First Time Franchise Buyer Should Follow", I listed all 49 "secrets" I disclosed throughout the book.

Add Book Hooks

Because the purpose of your book is to be an Ultimate Business Card, it is appropriate to sprinkle references to your work, how to get on your list, and how to reach you, throughout the book. Remember that the book's emphasis is to provide useful, actionable information for your readers, who may very well become your prospects. You'll see references to how to reach me scattered a few times throughout this book, mostly at the end of each chapter. Your "book hooks" can refer to your website, your list sign-up page, your Facebook page, your Twitter account, or your phone number.

Copy Editing

Now that the writing is nearly complete, it is time to have the book copy edited. A copy editor checks the spelling, grammar, punctuation, and terminology, and makes sure that place and people names are spelled correctly. Also, the copy editor will make sure captions on figures, illustrations, or tables are correct, and are correctly annotated. Good copy editors will also fact-check claims in the book for accuracy.

Create the Title

This task is intentionally placed after almost all of the writing is complete. The reason is that a title for the book often reveals itself during the development of the book, sometimes through the writing itself, or because the author and/or ghost-writer have a much clearer idea about the value of the book to the reader once the content is complete.

A good book title for your Ultimate Business Card should be easy to remember, and should quickly communicate the value that the book will bring to its reader. Here are some questions your title should answer.

- What problem does the book solve?

- Who is the reader?

- What is unique about your promise?

- Is the promise of the book obvious?

- Does it evoke curiosity?

- Is the title easy to remember?

- Optional: Can you get the URL for your title?

One of the non-fiction best sellers on Amazon right now is a book whose title is "How to Talk So Kids Will Listen & Listen So Kids Will Talk". You can see that this title does a great job of answering nearly all the questions. The "problem" is getting kids to listen and talk. The "reader" is a parent or teacher. What is unique is getting both the reader and kids to listen and talk. The title does evoke curiosity and it is easy to remember.

If your title is available as a URL, you may want to go ahead and buy it for a year, and then think about adding an Ultimate Business Card website that reinforces the messaging in the book, and can further stimulate sales. See more in the section on Create a Website.

Layout and Formatting

This step, often call interior design in the publishing industry, is a critical step in getting your book published. For many people, formatting your document for printing on CreateSpace and on KDP is the most tedious and challenging task in the whole process. There are books, articles, templates, and programs that have been written about this topic, so this isn't meant to be the ultimate how-to guide, but I'll provide enough detail using Microsoft® Word 2010 that will produce a reasonable result. There are a nearly infinite number of combinations of variables, and there is no single right way, and there are also many ways to get to the same result.

Select Trim Size. There are many choices available in CreateSpace for your finished book size, also known as trim size, but I recommend 6" x 9". That just seems to be the right size for a non-fiction paperback book. If you will be initially working in Microsoft Word 2010, then your default document size is probably 8½" x 11". Click on the "Page Layout" tab, then click on "Size" and scroll down to "More Paper Sizes". Change the paper size to 6" x 9", then select "Apply to Whole Document" in the selection box at the bottom of the page, and click OK, as follows:

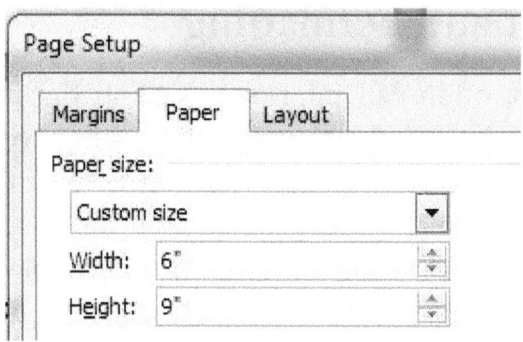

Figure 1: Page Setup

Important Note 1: If your screen dimensions are wide enough, your 6x9 image will show up two pages wide. You can also force this by going to the "View" tab, and then clicking on the "Two Pages" icon. What's important to note here is that these pages are reversed. That is, the page that shows up on the right will be printed on the left, and vice versa. This is just a function of Microsoft Word.

Important Note 2: Do NOT click the "Set as Default" button at the bottom of the page, or else all your new files will have these dimensions.

Set Formatting using Styles. There are many ways to get your fonts and paragraphs set, but I highly recommend using the Styles settings in Word. I find myself generally only using four styles: Normal,

Heading 1, Heading 2, and Heading 3. I recommend using Serif fonts, and I like Garamond 12, and Georgia 11, which this book uses. To get to these settings, go to the "Home" tab, and right click on the styles you want to set, then click the "Modify..." menu item.

Here is my set up for "Normal":

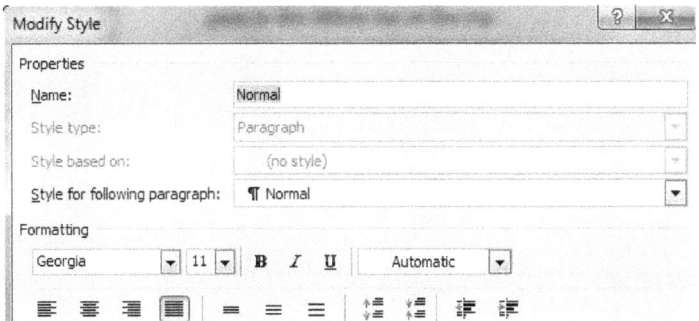

Figure 2: Style

Notice I selected Georgia, font size 11, and clicked on the "Justify" icon. I think justified text produces a more polished look to our books.

Next, click on the "Format" box in the lower left hand corner of the screen, and choose "Paragraph..." Here is my set up:

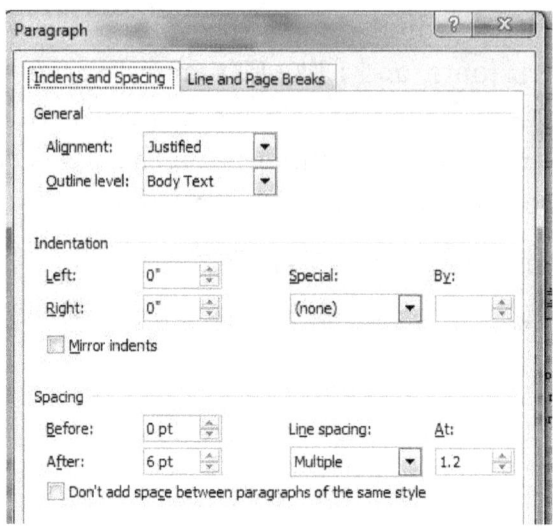

Figure 3: Paragraph Style

Notice that I don't do any indentation, and I have a spacing of 6 pts after each paragraph, and a line spacing of 1.2. Again, I like the look this gives to non-fiction books, but you are welcome to try any combination you think will make your book look just the way you want it.

My set up for "Heading 1", which I use for chapter titles, is 22 pt Georgia Bold, left justified, with spacing after of 108 pts, which emphasizes the chapter title.

My set up for "Heading 2" is 18 pt Georgia Bold, left justified, with spacing before of 24 pts, and after of 6 pts.

My set up for "Heading 3" is 14 pt Georgia Bold, left justified, with spacing before of 0 pts, and after of 6 pts.

Once you get these styles set up, select your text, or your chapter titles, or your sub-headings, and simply click the appropriate style. That way, if you want to make a universal change throughout your book, you just have to click the "Modify" button for that style, make the change, and it propagates throughout the book.

Create Section 1 for Title Page through Table of Contents. You'll want to make this Section 1, and then place a section break after the Table of Contents. The Title Page at the beginning doesn't need a page number, so the first thing you'll want to do is to click in the footer section, and the following menu will appear in the ribbon bar at the top:

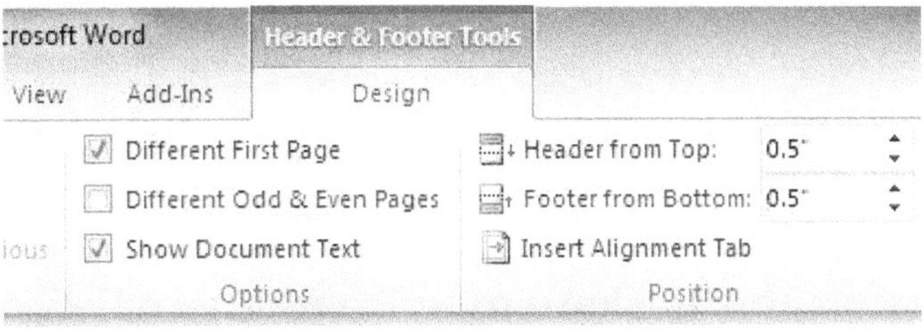

Figure 4: Modify Footer

Check the Different First Page checkbox, then I recommend setting the Header from Top and Footer from Bottom to .5". Delete the page number at the bottom of the first page if one shows up in the footer.

After that, click on "Page Number" then choose "Page Number Format…" Set the pagination to Roman Numerals in the drop-down menu, and set start to "i", as shown below.

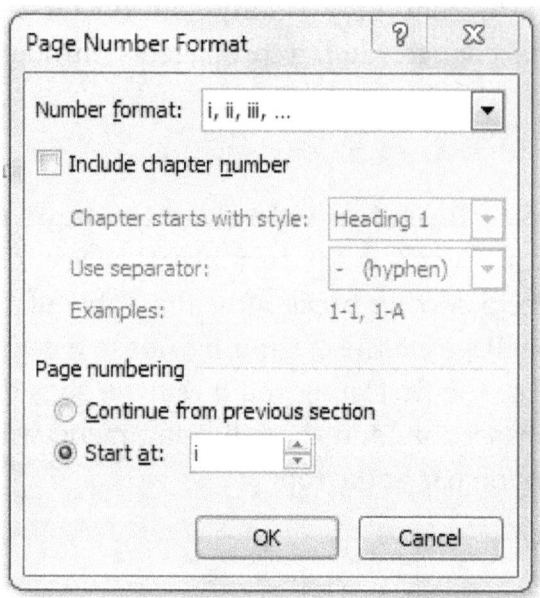

Figure 5: Page Number Format Section 1

Create Table of Contents. To create your ToC, click on the "References" tab, then the "Table of Contents" icon on the far left of the ribbon, and scroll down to and click on "Insert Table of Contents". You'll get the following screen:

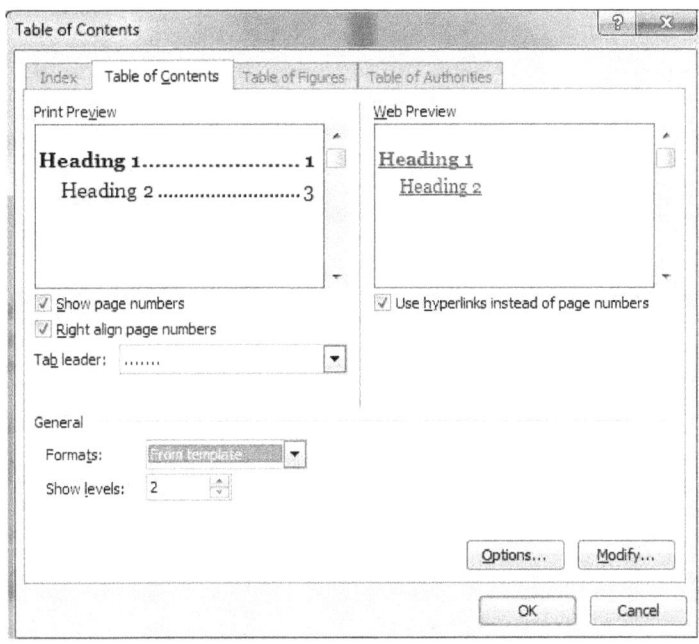

Figure 6: Table of Contents

I recommend that you go two levels deep in your ToC: it provides more detail about what is in your book, but not too much if you've used three or four heading styles. You can modify the appearance of each level by clicking on the "Modify..." button at the bottom right of the screen.

Set Main Text (Section 2) Pagination. At the end of the Table of Contents, create a Section Break, which will give you Section 2. Insert a couple lines after your ToC, and then click on the "Page Layout" tab, then click on the "Breaks" dropdown, then in the "Section Breaks" section, click on "Next page". Section 2 will now be created.

Now, double-click in the footer, and the "Header and Footer Toolbar" will appear. Click on the "Page Number" icon, then click on "Format Page Numbers", and you will get the following dialog box:

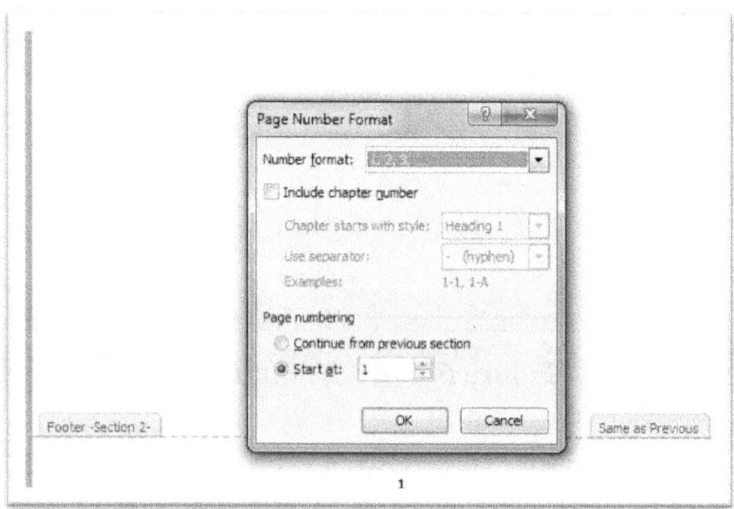

Figure 7: Page Number Format Section 2

Change the Number format to "1,2,3," and under "Page numbering", click the "Start at:" radio button, and start at 1. Now your main book content will start at Page 1.

Get Early Reviews

Now is the time to get some first reviews. Do your best to get a draft copy of your book into the hands of a few potential readers, usually people who know, like, and trust you, and get them to write a brief review (35-70 words), which you can use either on the inside or on the cover of the book. Most reviewers will be flattered that you asked them for a review, and savvy reviewers will understand that publicizing their name and company in your book could also be good for their business. If you want to spend the money, contract with Kirkus Indie or Foreword Clarion to write an objective serious review. Or you could pay writers on Fiverr or one of the other free-lancer sites to write reviews for you, but be careful not to get too many gushing over-the-top reviews this way, or it could end up backfiring. By the way, I do NOT recommend that you get paid reviews on Amazon once your book is published. There are better ways to get reviews once your book is published, which I will discuss later.

Design Front & Back Covers

While it is true that you can't judge a book by its cover, your cover will often convey the first impression to your reader, so you want it to be professional. Unless you are a graphics pro, this task is best left to specialists. The good news is that there are many artists who will design a great looking cover for you relatively inexpensively and also fairly quickly. You can find them on LinkedIn, eLance, oDesk, and even Craigslist.

Here are the items you will need to communicate to your cover designer:

- **Impression**. Tell the designer what you want the cover to communicate to the reader: e.g. exciting, solid professionalism, quirky, fun, evocative, etc. Tell the designer a little about your prospective readers and your purpose.

- **Images**. If you have an image or images you want to use, such as a photo of yourself or one of your works, be sure to include a high-res version.

- **Color**. If you have a strong preference on the colors you want on the cover, let the designer know up front.

- **Title**. To go on the front cover.

- **Subtitle**. To go on the front cover.

- **Exact author name**. To go on the front cover.

- **Spine width**. White (not cream) pages in CreateSpace are .002252 inches per page, and the book must be at least 137 pages long, or about 25,000 words without a lot of images, in order to be able to add text to the spine.

- **Spine text**. Generally the title and the author, if your spine width is wide enough (see above). Otherwise blank.

- **Blurb(s)**. These are the brief reviews I discussed earlier. You should have no more than six. Generally on the back cover, but optionally one brief one on the front.

- **Book summary**. On the back, useful for the reader.

- **About the author**. Back cover, to build branding and credibility. Be sure to include a high-res color photo.

- **ISBN barcode**. If you use CreateSpace, they will insert your ISBN barcode in the lower right corner of the back cover. The designer needs to leave a 1 ½" x 2" space here.

- **Dimensions**. Note: if you choose CreateSpace and a trim size of 6" x 9", you need to add 1/8" all around in order to accommodate a bleed, which is when a color extends to the edge of the page.

- **Kindle cover**. For highest quality, Kindle recommends a cover that is 1563 pixels on the shortest side and 2500 pixels on the longest side, which is a ratio of 1:1.6. Your graphics designer should know this already if they have designed Kindle covers before.

Proofreading

Proofreading is the final line of defense against typos in your book. Even though your book has been copy edited, there may be misspellings, or duplicate words that were missed, or other minor errors which a good proofreader will catch.

I think this is a very important step. It surprises me how many errors I find in many self-published works, and these errors reflect negatively on the author. It suggests to me that the author is either careless and doesn't pay attention to detail (not a good thing for a professional), or is just poorly educated or too cheap to have their book carefully edited.

I recommend that you budget a total of about $10-20 per thousand words for copy editing and proofreading by a professional.

Production Editing

Production editing is the process of formatting the finished book for each medium you are going to send to the printer. Here, I am assuming you are going to use CreateSpace and Kindle initially, so you'll want two different versions of your Word document. Remember that the Kindle version will not need any pagination, so be sure to create a version of your manuscript that removes the pagination.

Choose Pricing

Remember that research you did at the beginning this project? Now is the time to pull that research out and review books that are generally in the same market as yours, and decide how you want to be positioned in your market with respect to pricing. It's entirely up to you. You can price your Kindle book at $0.99 to $9.99, and you can price your paperback at nearly anything you want. You probably don't need to spend a great deal of time on this if your main purpose is to use your book as your Ultimate Business Card, since you'll be mostly giving away copies. I like to price my Kindle books from $2.99 to $8.99, but this pricing should be part of your marketing strategy, and I recommend pricing paperbacks from $7.99 to $14.99.

Set Up Accounts

Now it's time to set up your accounts in both CreateSpace and Kindle Direct Publishing (KDP).

CreateSpace Account Setup

Go to http://createspace.com and click the "Sign Up" link, enter your name, a password, and your email address. Note: at this time, this account is NOT automatically linked to your KDP account, even though both entities are owned by Amazon.

Once you are signed up, you'll have to set up your account for receiving your royalty payment. Be sure to think this through carefully: do you want to receive your payments in a business account or your personal account? It might be a good time to discuss this with your accountant.

Note: If you want to receive payments into a business account, be sure to set this up beforehand, including getting an EIN. If you are going to take payments personally, then you can use your Social Security number.

You'll also have to set up a billing account in order to pay for the copies of the books that you order.

KDP Account Setup

Go to http://kdp.amazon.com to set up your KDP account. In this case, you will be required to set up your account with your Amazon account. If you already have an Amazon account you'd like to use to publish under, you can enter that information. Or, you can sign up for a new Amazon account. You will have to provide your name, address, tax information, bank account information where you want your royalties deposited, and the international marketplaces where you'd like to have your book distributed.

After you have your CreateSpace and KDP accounts set up, you are ready to upload your content.

Upload Your Content and Publish!

You'll want to start with your CreateSpace account. Sign in to your account, and you'll be at your Member Dashboard. Click "Add New Title." At this point, you'll see four main categories of tasks:

- Setup
- Review
- Distribute
- Sales and Marketing

Under the "Setup" tab, you'll enter your title and a number of other details, the ISBN number, the interior, and the cover. The interior is your Word file, converted to pdf. You can either print to a pdf program, or you can save the document as a pdf document. You'll then upload your cover, which hopefully has been properly formatted. CreateSpace will check right away, and let you know.

The next part is "Review," which is where you'll be able to see a virtual copy of your book. Look through the copy and see if you need to make changes. If you do, you'll need to make changes in your manuscript, and then re-upload the file.

Once you are satisfied with the electronic version of your book, it's time to order your proof. Go ahead and splurge a little bit and order at least two: one for you and one for a friend or advisor who is helping you with your book. It will take a couple of days for the proof to arrive, and when it does, your heart rate will go up a little bit as you see your very own book with your name on the cover!

While you're waiting for your proof to arrive, you can fill out the "Distribute" tasks. First up, you'll be able to select the "Channels," which gives you the capability to have the book available throughout the world. There isn't much reason not to select all of these channels.

Next up is pricing. Select the price you chose earlier. Next is the Cover Finish, which can be either glossy or matte. I generally recommend a glossy finish.

Next is "Description," where you have 4,000 characters to describe your book. This is where you also select your BISAC code, and an author bio of up to 2,500 characters. BISAC codes are industry standard categories that help classify your book, and a list of current codes is provided in the CreateSpace interface.

Finally, you have the option of converting your content directly to your KDP account. I recommend that you follow this process, but that you wait until you have had the opportunity to review your hard copy first.

After you get your proof copy, review it thoroughly. When you are satisfied with it, it's time to approve the proof, and if all your other information is filled out, your book will be available to order online within hours.

Next up is to get your book onto Kindle. You can get there by having CreateSpace upload the content into Kindle from your CreateSpace account, or you can go to your KDP account and upload your content there. My experience is that it is better to avoid the CreateSpace interface, as it doesn't do a great job of formatting the content for Kindle. It's more work to create another Word document for your Kindle book, but it is worth it.

When you enter your information in KDP, there will be a number of other selections you'll need to make.

Your first choice will be whether or not to choose to market your book through KDP Select. KDP Select gives Amazon the exclusive rights on the electronic version of your book for a period of 90 days. During that time, you can reduce the price of the Kindle version down to $0.99 for up to 5 days, or you can price it for free during that period. Authors often take advantage of this opportunity to promote downloads and purchases of their book, hoping for it to break into the "Best Seller" ranks in their category. If you aren't planning to sell your ebook through other channels such as Nook, then I advise signing up for KDP Select. It's a rolling 90-day commitment that you can exit from at the end of any 90-day period.

After that, you'll be asked to verify your rights to publish your book, select the categories and keywords for your book, and the age range of your target audience. You'll also be asked whether to invoke Digital Rights Management. I recommend that you do NOT invoke this option, as it can reduce the end-user experience. Given that you are writing this book as an Ultimate Business Card, you aren't relying on sales of the book for income, so you don't need to be too concerned about digital rights. You still do have the copyright, however, which you can still enforce after the fact if you discover that someone has plagiarized your book.

The next sections deal with Rights and Pricing. Generally, you want to check the Worldwide Rights radio box, then set your KDP Royalty and Pricing. You'll want to select the 70% option, and then you can set worldwide pricing. It's easiest to just click the option that sets the pricing based on the US pricing.

The final choices are opting-in to the Kindle MatchBook program, which enables anyone who buys the printed version to get the Kindle version for $2.99, and the Lending option, which enables Kindle owners to borrow the book. I recommend that you opt in to both these programs.

Book Publishing Action Plan

If you now have a burning desire to get your book published, it will probably take a well-defined action plan to insure you get the book written and published in a reasonable timeframe. Here are a couple of templates that you can use with some of my best estimates for the resources – hours, duration, and dollars - you'll need to get the book published. Of course, the first choice you'll need to make is how much of the process you want to do yourself, versus hiring professionals to help you. Here are my estimates, based on my professional experience. Of course, your results may vary!

Book Publishing Action Plan - Do It Yourself

		Estimated	Hours	Days		Cost	
Step	Action	Min	Max	Min	Max	Min	Max
1	Set goal date	0.0	0.5				
2	Define purpose	0.5	1.0				
3	Create promotion plan	0.5	1.0				
4	Research	0.5	2.0				
5	Table of Contents	1.0	3.0	1	1		
6	Write Content (15,000 words)	25.0	40.0	30	60		
7	Add images/illustrations	0.0	10.0	2	7		$1,000
8	Write front and back matter	2.0	5.0	1	7		
9	Web Page/list /book hooks	2.0	8.0	1	7		$1,000
10	Edit content	8.0	12.0	3	7		$2,000
11	Select title	0.5	1.0	0	0		
12	Format content	2.0	10.0	1	3		$500
13	Get reviews	2.0	4.0	3	7		$500
14	Design covers	1.0	2.0	3	7	$250	$800
15	Final editing	5.0	15.0	1	3		$1,000
16	Choose pricing	0.5	1.0				
17	Set up publishing accounts	1.0	2.0	1	1		
18	Upload content, get proof	1.0	2.0	4	4		
19	Publish						
20	Promote						
	Totals	52.5	119.5	51	114	$250	$6,800

Figure 8: DIY Action Plan

Book Publishing Action Plan - Done for You

Step	Action	Estimated		Hours		Days		Cost	
		Min	Max	Min	Max	Min	Max	Min	Max
1	Set goal date	0.0	0.5						
2	Define purpose	0.5	1.0						
3	Create promotion plan	0.5	1.0						
4	Research	0.0	0.0						
5	Table of Contents	1.0	3.0	1	1			$0	$250
6	Write Content (15,000 words)	2.0	5.0	3	30			$3,000	$7,500
7	Add images/illustrations	0.0	0.5	2	7				$1,000
8	Write front and back matter	0.5	1.0	1	7			$500	$1,000
9	Web Page/list /book hooks	0.0	0.5	1	7			$500	$1,000
10	Edit content	0.0	4.0	3	7			$500	$2,000
11	Select title	0.5	1.0	0	0				
12	Format content	0.0	0.0	1	3			$250	$500
13	Get reviews	1.0	2.0	3	7			$250	$500
14	Design covers	1.0	2.0	3	7			$250	$800
15	Final editing	0.0	2.0	1	3			$500	$1,000
16	Choose pricing	0.5	1.0						
17	Set up publishing accounts	0.5	1.0	1	1			$100	$200
18	Upload content, get proof	0.0	0.0	4	4			$250	$500
19	Publish								
20	Promote								
	Totals	8.0	25.5	24	84			$6,100	$16,250

Figure 9: Done for You Action Plan

To get updates to this book, access to new videos that will show you how to implement the strategies in this book, and to reach me personally, visit:

- *www.UltimateBusinessCardGuide.com or*
- *text UBC to 58885 or*
- *text your name and email to (858) 683-8820*

5 | Promote Your Book

Create Lead Capture Campaign

Imagine what it would be like if you had a list of all the clients you have worked with in the past, the people interested in your expertise and who want to send prospective clients to you, and of course prospective new clients as well. Wouldn't it be great to send them targeted content on a regular basis, information that could help them solve problems that you know how to fix? Then, when they are ready for your products or services, you are top of mind, and end up earning their business.

You've heard it before, and it's true: besides your valuable skills, the most important asset you can develop is your list. And in order to establish and maintain this list, you'll need to have a combination of technologies that enable you to easily collect information from those who want to be on your list, then send communications to them in a variety of media, including email, text, voicemail, podcast, and video, that they can see, hear, read on almost any device anywhere in the world.

Your new book – your Ultimate Business Card – should be a lead magnet for you. Just as you see in this book, there should multiple ways for readers to reach out to you if they like what they are reading.

There are many services out there that provide various levels of list management, including Constant Contact®, iContact®, GetResponse®, aWeber®, and so on.

I provide this lead management service to my clients using a state-of-the-art system to which I subscribe.

I highly recommend that you subscribe to a system, then sprinkle invitations throughout your book for readers to reach you if they like what you're offering. The system should include a landing page where people can give you their information and get on your list.

Reach Out to Past Clients

Be sure to let your past clients know about your book, even if you haven't been in touch with them for a while. Letting your past clients know about the book may stimulate them to re-engage with and also to refer you to their circle of contacts who may need your services. Offer to send your book to your past clients for free as a thank-you for their past business – this builds goodwill, and will likely result in new business.

Promote to Your Social Network

Once your book is published, let everyone in your social circle know about it! One suggestion is to offer your book for free to anyone who is interested in the subject. If you have a copy of your book with you, trade the book for the person's contact information, or direct them to a landing page where they can request your book. If you belong to a business networking group, offer it there. Be sure to bring a couple of your books to each meeting, and trade them for getting people on your list. Also, be sure to mention your book in your online social media groups, especially LinkedIn and Facebook. And please be sure to get on a schedule to mention your book periodically in your online social networks, at least once a month.

Create a Press Release

Although the power of press releases has been declining in recent years, it can be marginally helpful to create a press release for your book, and you can use both free and paid sites to distribute your release. Here are some suggestions:

Free PR sites

- PRLog.org

- PR.com

- i-newswire.com

Paid PR sites

- PRNewswire.com

- PRweb.com

- BusinessWire.com

Send Lumpy Packages

You probably subscribe to a number of periodicals or websites that provide news about prospective clients. When you discover an article that focuses on a company or individual you think could be a prospective client, send them your book (autographed), preferably by FedEx®, and a cover letter offering to get together to help them. Alternatively, you could send the book directly through Amazon. In this day and age where it is very difficult to get anyone's attention, getting a "lumpy package" can be a winning strategy.

Offer to Speak to Targeted Groups

You are probably aware of networking groups or conferences that would welcome your expertise during one of their gatherings. If you are a wealth manager, you might want to reach out to groups of accountants or lawyers who cater to high net worth individuals, and who would benefit from hearing from you, and if they like what they hear, would refer clients to you.

Create and Publish Short Videos

YouTube, owned by Google, has become the second most popular search engine, and while YouTube in general is populated by a lot of goofy and/or entertainment related content, videos posted on your branded YouTube channel (and other sites such as Vimeo® and DailyMotion®) can be very effective in getting your message distributed.

A very effective strategy for many experts is to create a series of 10-20 short (1-5 minutes each) videos that address the most frequently asked questions about your subject matter. When people can see you talk about your subject, and/or hear you through a podcast, and then read your content in the form of a book, you will have established a bond by the time they reach out to you.

Again, creating these videos doesn't necessarily need to be overly complicated or expensive, but it should be done well, especially the audio. You can create good quality videos with a simple webcam. Here again, you might benefit from having a professional help you create these. Once they start working, consider staying on a schedule to continue producing these videos.

Create a Podcast

It's estimated that roughly 90 million Americans commute, and that the average commute time is 30 minutes. More and more people are listening to podcasts during their commutes, so producing a podcast of your content can be an effective way of getting your message out. It's fairly easy to convert your short videos to a podcast format, and offer it up on iTunes® and other podcasting networks. This would complete the cycle of having you seen, heard, and read on almost any device, at any time, and in any place throughout the world.

To get updates to this book, access to new videos that will show you how to implement the strategies in this book, and to reach me personally, visit:

- *www.UltimateBusinessCardGuide.com or*
- *text UBC to 58885 or*
- *text your name and email to (858) 683-8820*

6 | Take Action Now

Several years ago, I attended a seminar where the leader said: "If you provide a product or service that helps other people improve their lives, you have an ethical obligation to communicate that value as widely as you can." I think there's truth in that.

If you have a gift, if you have expertise and knowledge that can help others, please share your message. It is likely that someone who receives your message will change their life. Could what you know help someone increase their wealth or well-being, save a relationship, even save a life? If so, have you done everything you can to get that message to those who need it? And the benefit to you is that getting your message out there could change your own life for the better, too.

We live in a time when it is so much easier to have your message reach the world: locally, regionally, nationally, and internationally, and through any medium. My purpose in writing this book is to stimulate you to start down a path that will enable more people in the world to benefit from your expertise. Take action now!

To get updates to this book, access to new videos that will show you how to implement the strategies in this book, and to reach me personally, visit:

- *www.UltimateBusinessCardGuide.com or*
- *text UBC to 58885 or*
- *text your name and email to (858) 683-8820*

Disclaimers

OK, here is the fine print. I think most of this is pretty obvious, but my intention is to make it crystal clear.

Income Disclaimer

This document contains business strategies, marketing methods and other business advice that, regardless of my own results and experience, may not produce the same results (or any results) for you. I make absolutely no guarantee, expressed or implied, that by following the advice below you will make any money or improve current profits, as there are many factors and variables that come into play regarding any given business.

Primarily, results will depend on the nature of your product or business model, the conditions of the marketplace, the experience of the individual, and situations and elements that are beyond your control.

As with any business endeavor, you assume all risk related to investment and money based on your own discretion and at your own potential expense.

Liability Disclaimer

By reading this document, you assume all risks associated with using the advice given below, with a full understanding that you, solely, are responsible for anything that may occur as a result of putting this information into action in any way, and regardless of your interpretation of the advice.

You further agree that neither I nor my company can be held responsible in any way for the success or failure of your business as a result of the information presented in this book. It is your responsibility to conduct your own due diligence regarding the safe and successful operation of your business if you intend to apply any of our information in any way to your business operations.

Terms of Use

You are given a non-transferable, "personal use" license to this product. You cannot distribute it or share it with other individuals.

Also, there are no resale rights or private label rights granted when purchasing this book. In other words, it's for your own personal use only.

Affiliate Relationships Disclosure

I make a number of references in this book about vendors or programs that I use or recommend. I have no affiliate relationship at all with any vendor I reference, nor have any of them endorsed my book in any way.